NATIONAL GEOGRAPHIC

Winter Is Here

Sid Webb

The trees are bare.

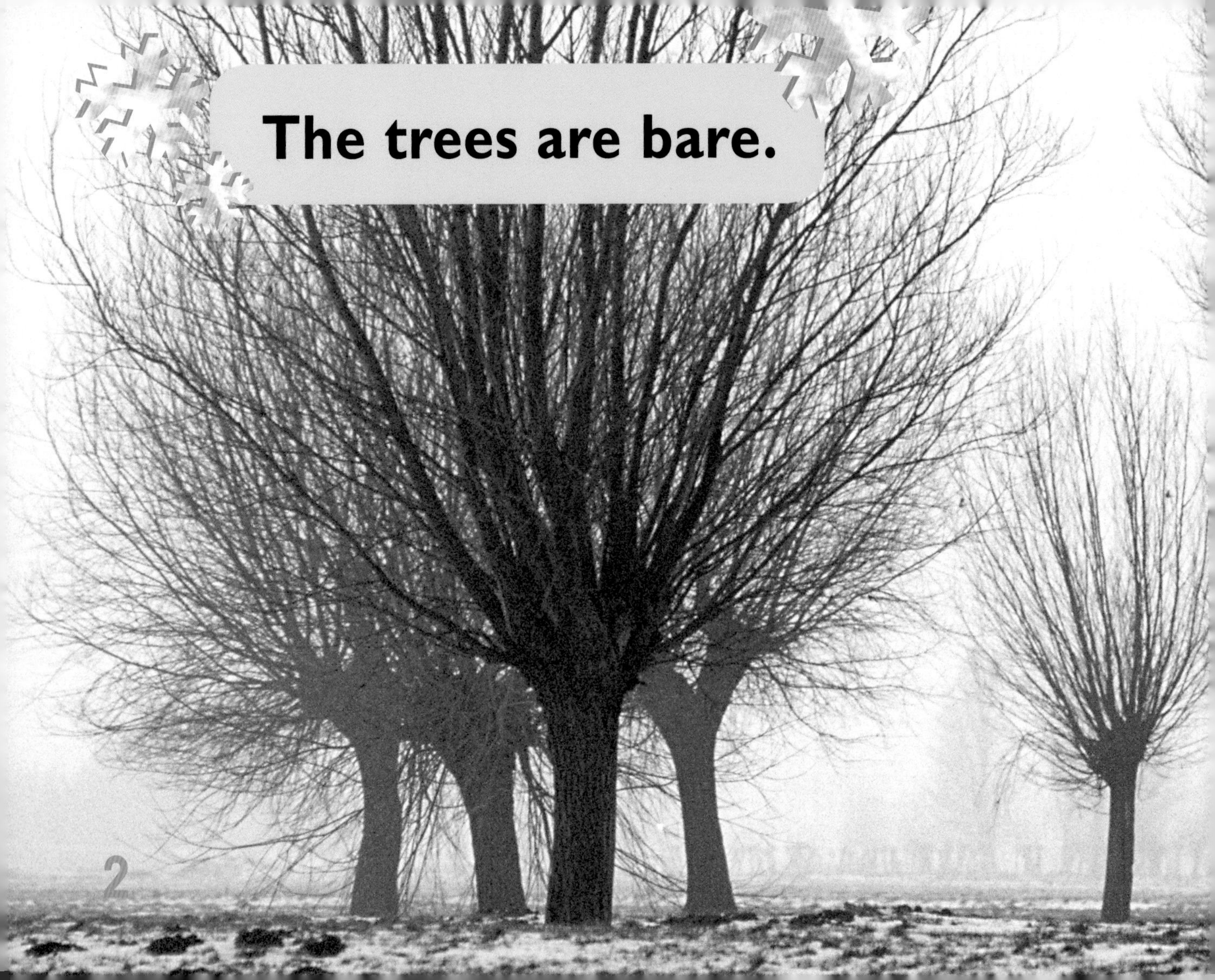

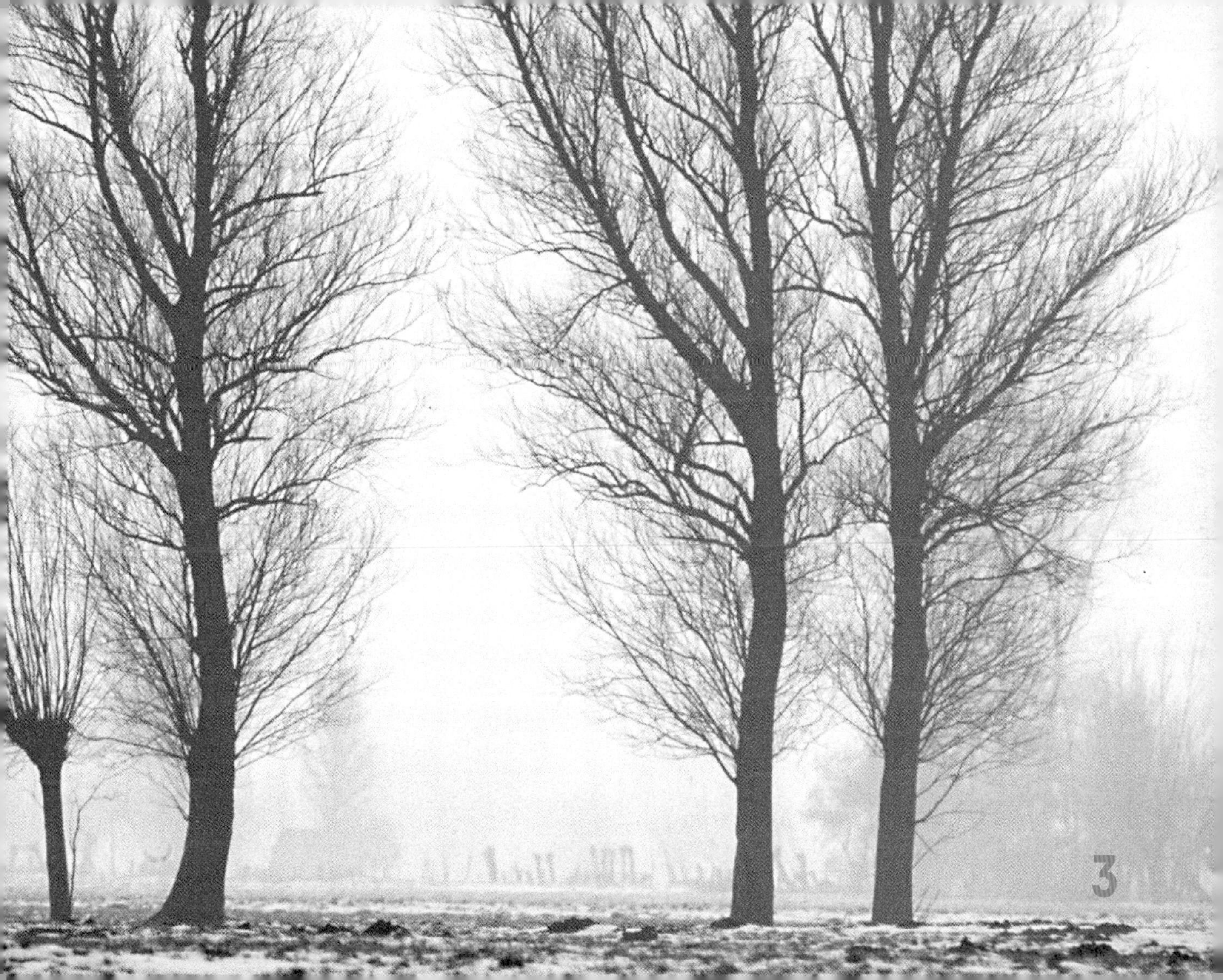

3

The air is cold.

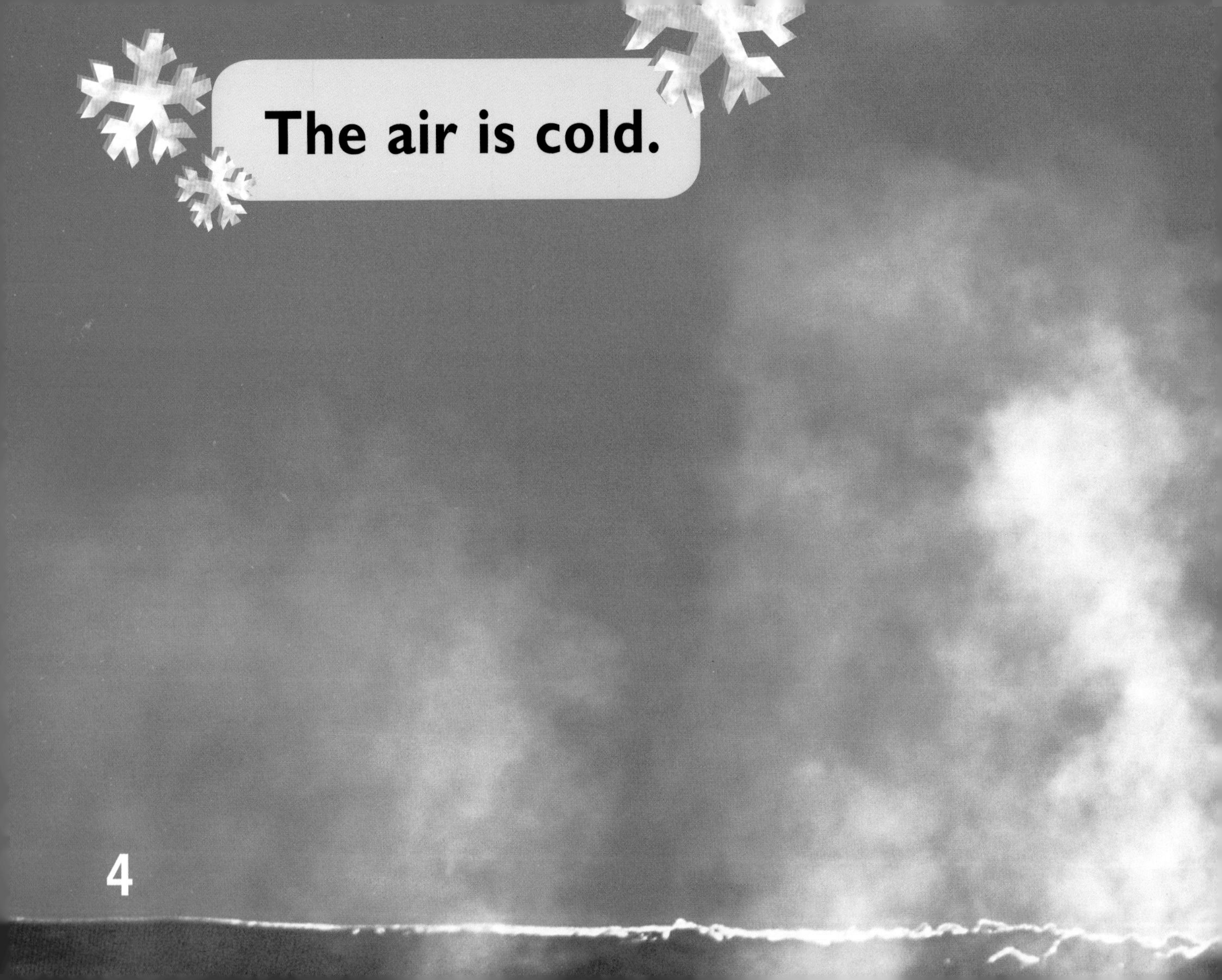

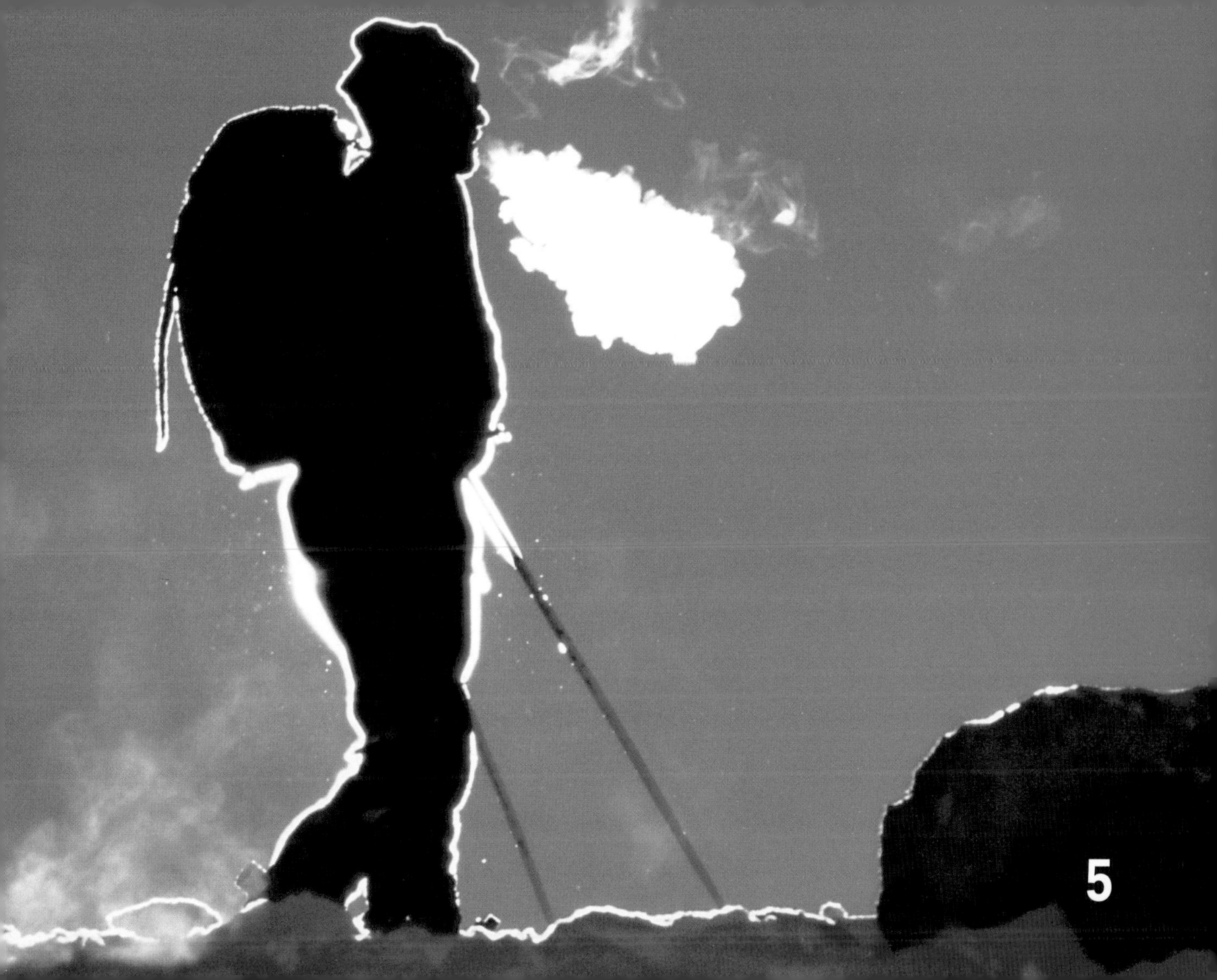

Snow falls from the sky.

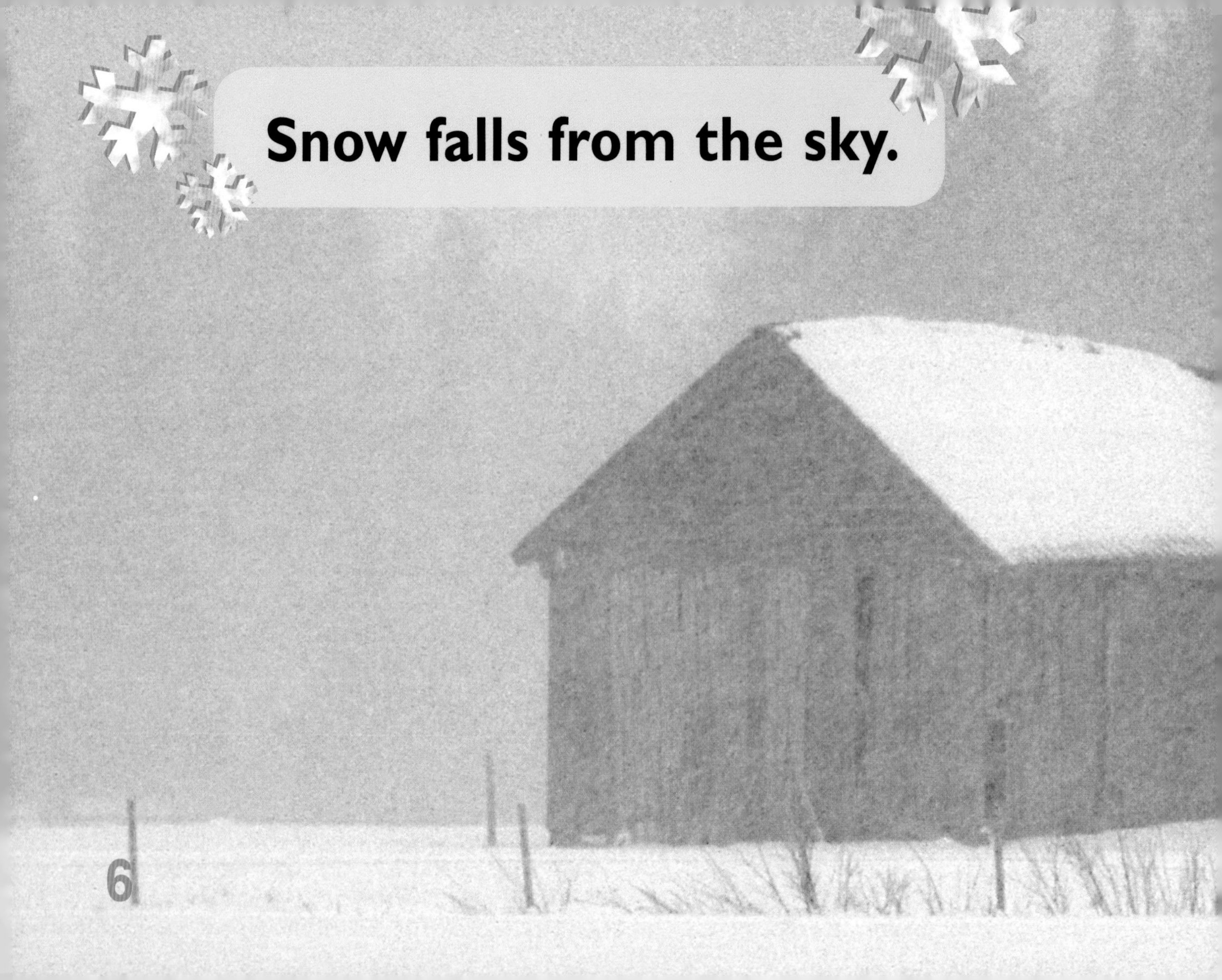

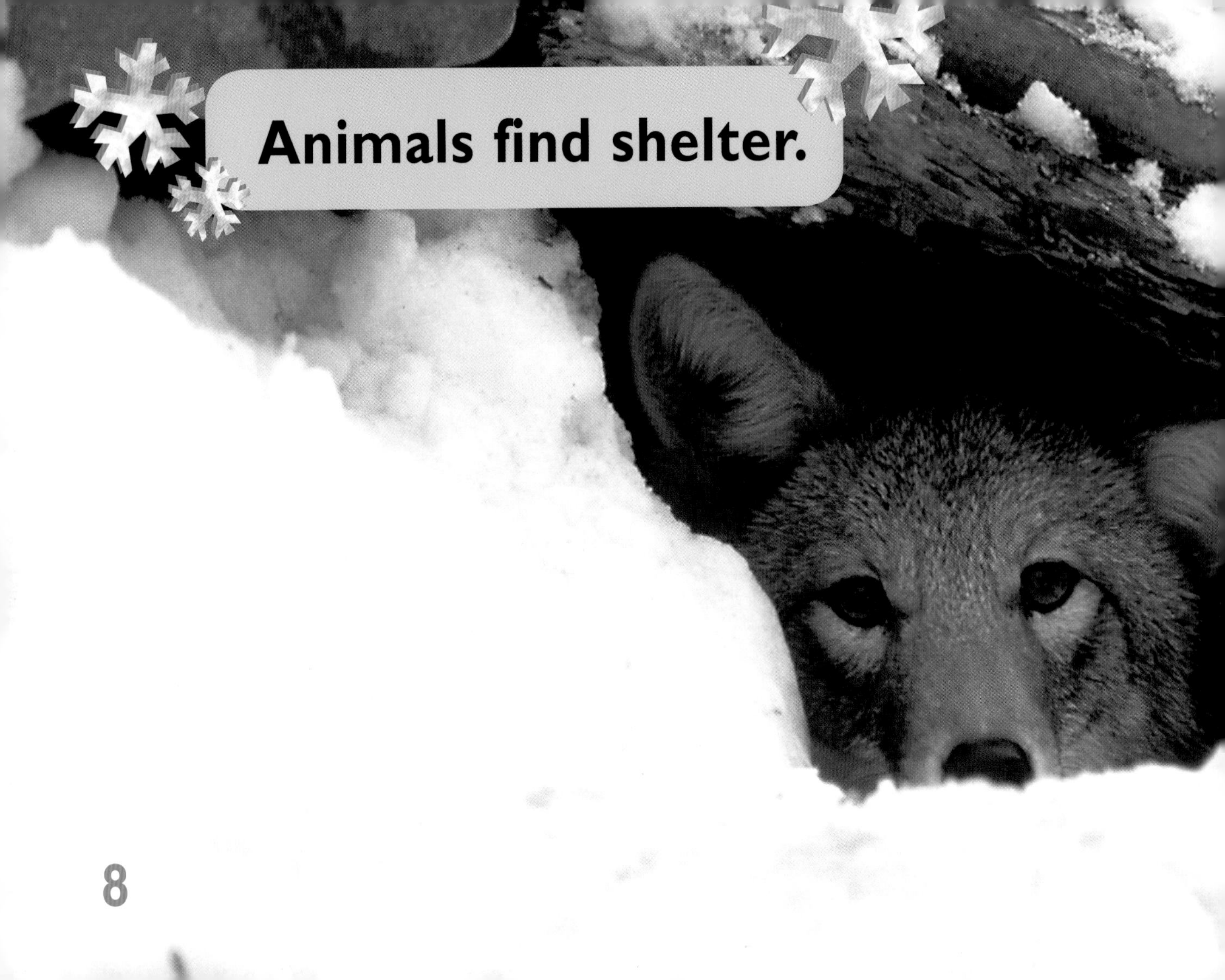

Animals find shelter.

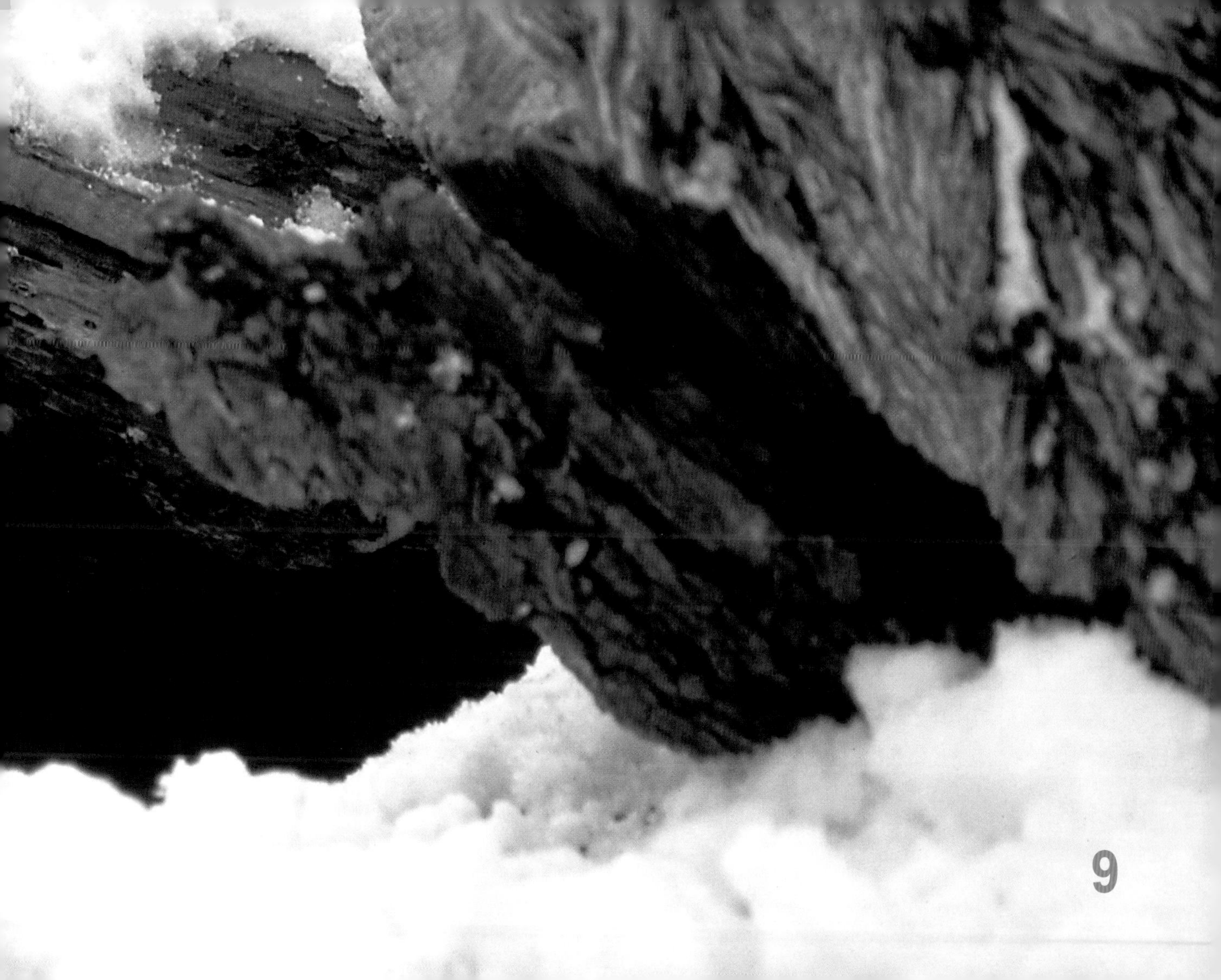

Ice freezes on the pond.

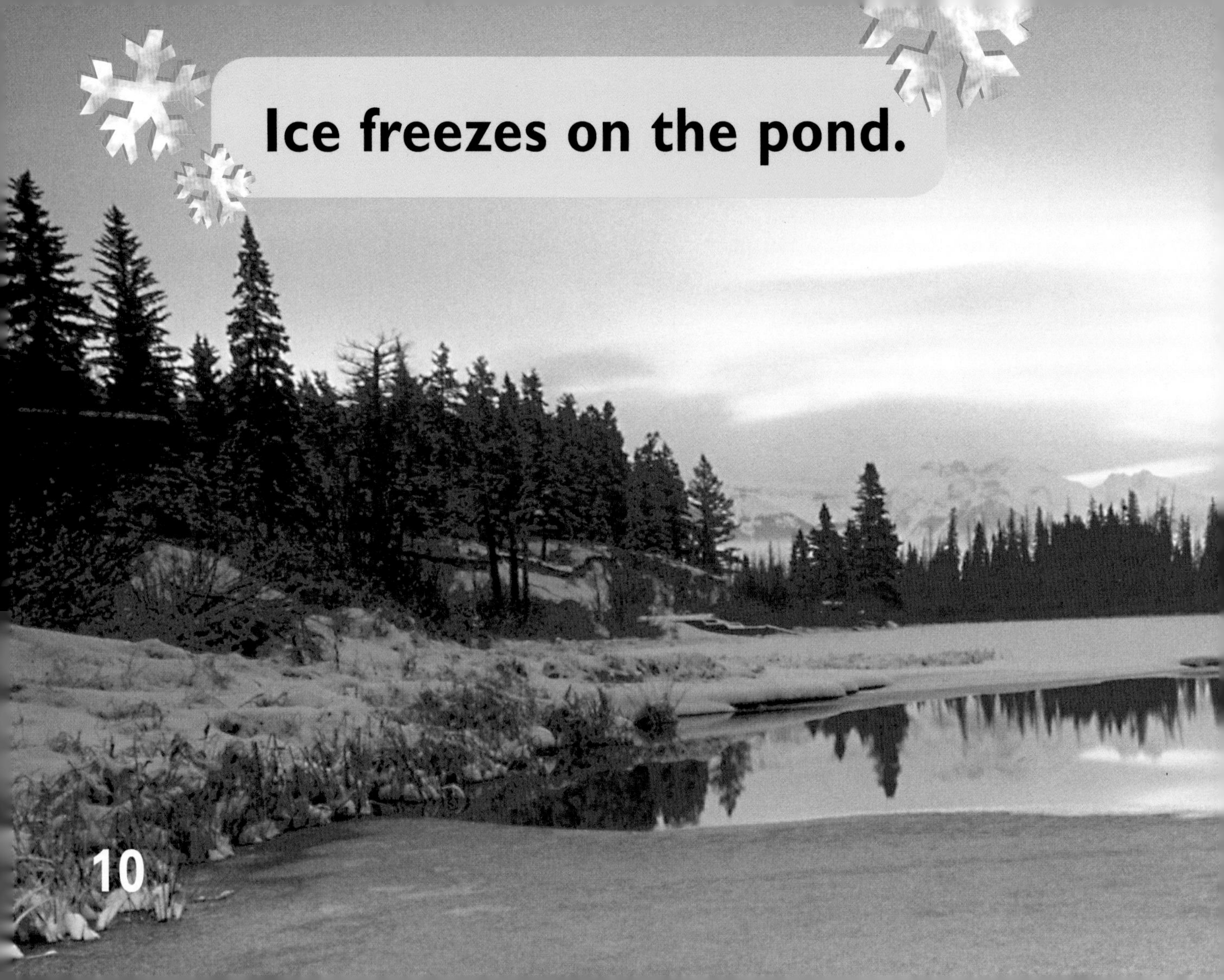

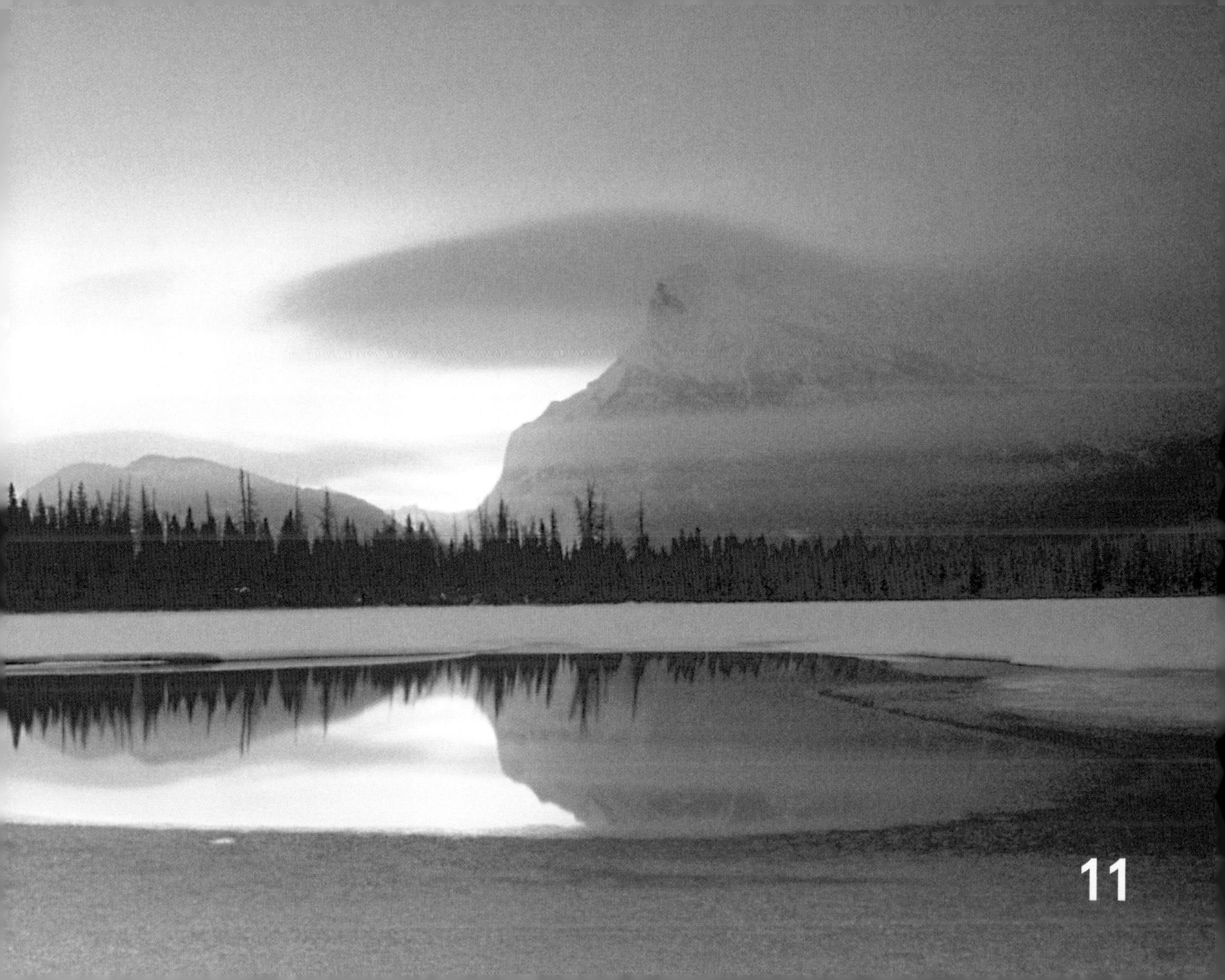

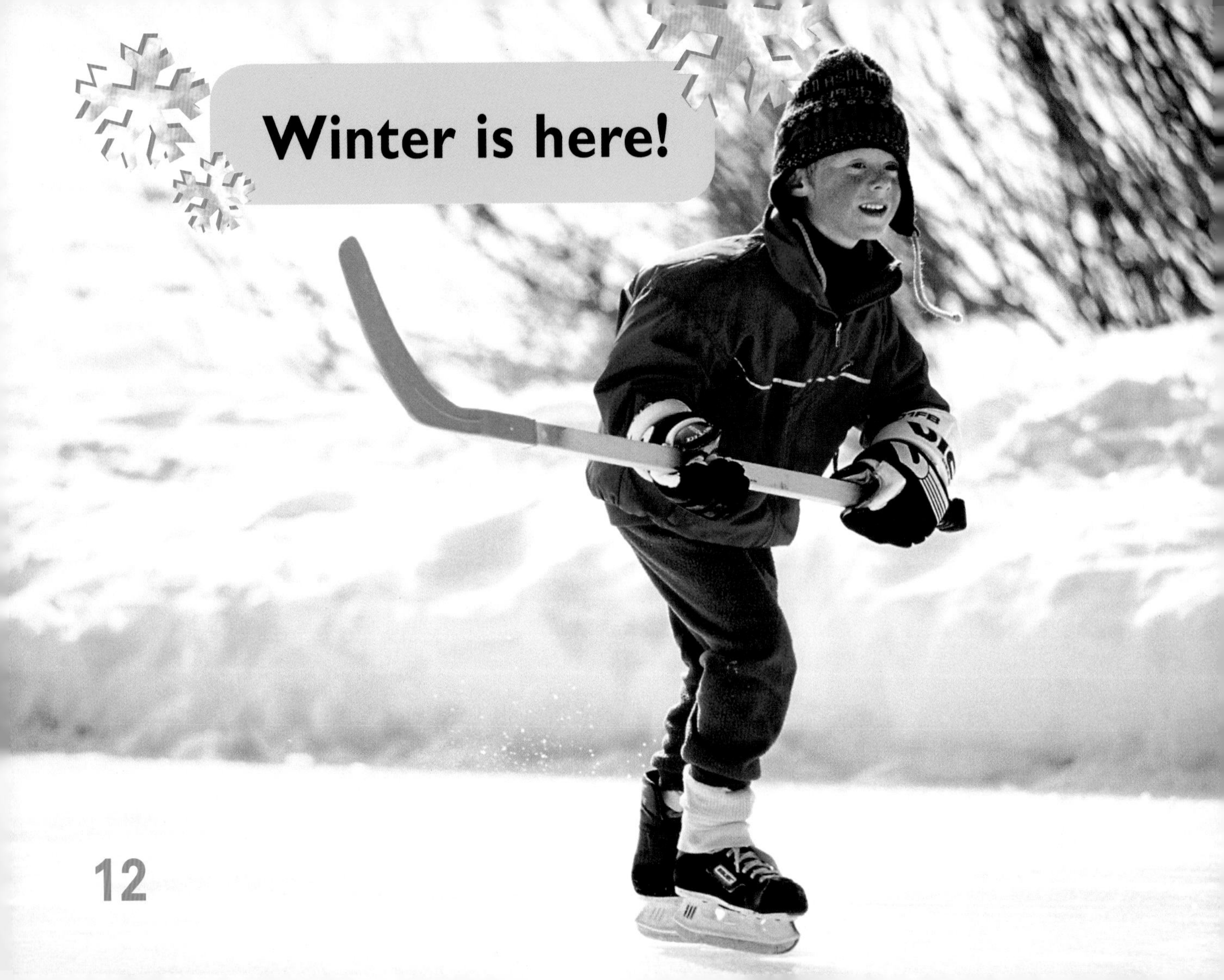

Winter is here!